Edvania

Higher E

Edvania Cristina C. Rodrigues da Silva

Higher Education and Teaching Quality

University Teaching

ScienciaScripts

Cover image: www.ingimage.com

This book is a translation from the original published under ISBN 978-620-2-40802-8.

Publisher:
Sciencia Scripts
is a trademark of
Dodo Books Indian Ocean Ltd. and OmniScriptum S.R.L publishing group

120 High Road, East Finchley, London, N2 9ED, United Kingdom
Str. Armeneasca 28/1, office 1, Chisinau MD-2012, Republic of Moldova, Europe

ISBN: 978-620-8-32554-1

To my parents, who tirelessly helped to shape me as a human being and a professional.

To my husband and daughter for their patience, care and love.

SUMMARY

INTRODUCTION

When we talk about continuing teacher training from a historical-social perspective, we take pedagogical practice as our basis and place the aim of this practice at getting students to master the knowledge accumulated historically by humanity. For students to be able to appropriate school knowledge in such a way as to become autonomous and critical, the teacher himself needs to be appropriating this knowledge and becoming increasingly autonomous and critical (MAZZEU, 1998). It was based on the assumption that human action is endowed with personal meanings and senses, within a dynamic context in which elements of the personal and professional history of students in constant formation are articulated.

In this sense, what prompted the development of this research, which is not limited in its relevance to this researcher's personal questions, concerns the way in which higher education teachers have been qualifying. I believe that this research can contribute to discussions about the qualification of higher education teachers and its importance for improving the quality of teaching at university.

One of the possibilities that is considered relevant is the exercise of research, which becomes fundamental in the training of educators, because according to Marafon (2001, 111), in carrying out research the future teacher experiences a fundamental academic experience, discovers himself as a researcher and becomes convinced that man at any age is endowed with curiosity and creative capacity. These characteristics should be explored in different ways, according to age, pushing the whole being towards knowledge. In this sense, what is being investigated here is whether higher education teachers are seeking adequate training for this profession.

When we talk about the continuing education of teachers from a historical-social perspective, we take pedagogical practice as our basis and place the aim of this practice at getting students to master the knowledge accumulated historically by humanity. In order for students to be able to appropriate school knowledge in such a way as to become autonomous and critical, teachers themselves need to be appropriating this knowledge and becoming increasingly autonomous and critical (MAZZEU, 1998).

In this way, the aim of this research was to investigate the type of professional training and qualification carried out by higher education teachers by verifying their initial training, analyzing the literature on the subject and understanding how professional qualification occurs among these higher education teachers, as well as verifying how this training reflects directly or indirectly on improving the quality of higher education and the training of the students they teach.

In order to achieve the objectives set out in this research and answer the questions raised at the beginning of this investigation, we used bibliographical research. It can be said that bibliographical research is the search for a problematization of the research project based on published references, analyzing and discussing cultural and scientific contributions. This is an excellent technique for

4

providing the researcher with theoretical background, knowledge and scientific training.

This book has been organized into four chapters, the first of which, **"DILEMAS ON TEACHING TRAINING"**, provides a historical overview of the professionalization of teachers throughout Brazil's educational history, as well as pointing out the crisis and overcoming of the identity of the teaching professional in this period, and dealing with the rise of higher education in Brazil. The second chapter, **"TEACHER QUALIFICATION"**, deals with the initial and continuing training of higher education teachers, pointing out the importance of qualification in the process of acquiring quality teaching. The third chapter, **"IMPROVING THE QUALITY OF HIGHER EDUCATION"**, discusses how teacher training can improve the quality of basic and higher education. In the fourth chapter, **"THE RESEARCH"**, the research is characterized and the path taken in the bibliographic analysis is pointed out. **"THE FINAL CONSIDERATIONS"** closes the book with some reflections on teacher training and the quality of higher education.

I would like to make it clear that this study is not limited to the subject at hand, but it is hoped that it can contribute to a process of constant reflection and transformation in the ways in which higher education teachers think about and conceive of teaching. I believe that higher education should be a place where people can experience significant experiences in their teaching practice, contributing to the transformation and improvement of teaching quality.

Chapter I

DILEMMAS ABOUT TEACHER TRAINING

Before we talk about teacher training in higher education, we'll give you a history of teacher training institutions from their beginnings around the 17th century until they arrived here in Brazil. According to Saviani (2008), this preoccupation with teacher training began with Comenius, and from then on, teacher training schools were created out of a concern to educate the lower classes, thus giving rise to the Normal Schools in Europe.

In order to talk about teacher training in Brazil, we first need to take a historical look at Brazilian education, from the arrival of the Jesuits to the present day. Brazilian education began with the arrival of the Jesuits in the 16th century, when the Indians, who were initially taught by adults and the father, began to be catechized and educated under a hierarchical and religious education. In the 18th century, with the introduction of public education by the Marquis of Pombal, the Jesuits, who had held a monopoly on Brazilian school education for two hundred years, were expelled from Brazil and replaced by priests from other religious orders and some lay people.

The new model of education was based on Enlightenment ideals that required individuals to understand their rights and duties, as well as the search for independent thought and discourse. It was also during this period that public education emerged, which was controlled by the state in Portugal, and in Brazil teachers began to receive payment for the work they did in teaching through regular classes.

Brazilian education only underwent more profound changes when the Portuguese Court came to Brazil in 1808. At that time, education was structured into primary schools, gymnasiums and universities, with the aim of implementing a national education system. But despite these structural changes in education, what was observed was a lack of sufficient teachers to meet the demand of students at the time and a lack of minimum organization for national education (GHIRALDELLI, 2006).

Due to this expansionist education policy, which focused on quantity rather than the quality of education professionals, the training of primary school teachers took on a terminal character, i.e. at the end of the course the student was qualified to work as a teacher, and within this reality, a huge contingent of teachers was trained to meet the interests of this policy of expanding Brazilian education. This ended up resulting in a devaluation of the teaching profession, especially that of teacher (OLIVEIRA, 1994).

Oliveira (1994) also tells us that the concern to train teachers occurred in Brazil explicitly after independence, when the need to organize popular education also arose. According to the same author, the promulgation of Decree 7.247, which instituted the freedom of primary and secondary education in the Court and higher education throughout the country, meant that people who did not have a teaching qualification could act as teachers, i.e. it was enough to think you were qualified to teach and you could put forward your ideas and use your own method. This law also pointed out that the teaching function was incompatible with public and administrative positions, which ended up de-characterizing the role of the teacher as a professional.

According to Saviani (2009), the training of teachers in Brazil went through several periods, in which we can identify: Intermittent trials of teacher training (1827-1890) began with the enactment of the Law of the Schools of First Letters, which placed demands on the didactic preparation of teachers through a method of mutual teaching, this period lasted until 1890 when the model of the Normal Schools prevailed, which advocated specific training. This period was marked by the Paulista Reform of the Normal School, which was annexed to the model school.

The Institutes of Education, created in 1932, had as their objective not only teaching, but also research, and were spheres for the cultivation of education. This period was marked by the reforms of Anisio Teixeira in the Federal District in 1932 and Fernando de Azevedo in Sao Paulo in 1933. Organization and implementation of Pedagogy and Degree Courses and consolidation of the normal schools model (1939-1971).

The same author tells us about the replacement of the Normal School by the Specific Teaching Qualification (1971-1996). Finally, the advent of Higher Education Institutes and Higher Normal Schools (1996-2006). And the new profile of the pedagogy course, bearing in mind that each of these periods has its own characteristics that stem from the changes that have taken place in society and in the way teaching is conceived.

Through this historical process of teacher training in the country over the last two centuries, it can be seen that despite successive changes in the way teacher training is oriented, there is still a lack of continuity in this process, as well as unsatisfactory approaches to important issues such as pedagogy and the precariousness of training policies.

Given all these points, it is worth analyzing the theoretical aspects in question here. Due to the need to train teachers on a large scale as a result of the democratization of elementary education in the 1970s, education systems had to organize themselves, opposing two models of teacher training: the cultural - cognitive content model and the pedagogical - didactic model.

In addition to teacher training models, a number of dilemmas have also been raised throughout Brazil's teaching history. It is important to remember that alongside these dilemmas and teacher training, other issues need to be discussed, such as salaries, decent working conditions and the working hours of teachers.

On this subject, Saviani tells us that:

> [...] the issue of teacher training cannot be dissociated from the problem of the working conditions that surround the teaching career, in which the issues of salaries and working hours must be addressed. In fact, precarious working conditions not only neutralize the action of teachers, even if they were well trained. These conditions also hinder good training, as they act as a disincentive to seek out teacher training courses and dedicate themselves to their studies. (SAVIANI, 2009, p. 153)

Once these issues are resolved, perhaps the teaching profession will become more attractive and more valued by other segments of society. According to the literature on the subject, teachers in higher education generally identify themselves through their area of expertise and not as teachers of the course they teach. Most university professors do not assume their teaching identity, and see it as a way of supplementing their salary, because according to Pimenta (2002), the title of professor alone suggests a lesser identity, since socially it seems to refer to primary school teachers.

This problem points to a fundamental question: what training have these professionals received?

We can begin our discussions on the training of higher education teachers with the thoughts of Isaia and Bolzan (2011), who report that these professionals have no prior or specific training. Most of the time, the start of their professional career is very fragile, as they take on teaching responsibilities based on natural models or mirror the masters they internalized in their initial training, combined with knowledge from a certain scientific field and practice as professionals in an activity other than teaching in higher education. The National Education Guidelines and Bases Law itself (9394/96) does not clearly state in any of its articles the main characteristics of university teachers, especially with regard to their didactic training.

From this perspective, Morosini (2000) tells us that:

> We have found university professors didactic training obtained in degree courses; others, who bring their professional experience into the classroom; and still others, with no professional or didactic experience, who come from specialization and/or stricto sensu courses. Until then, the

defining factor in selecting teachers was scientific competence (p.11).

The same author (2000) reveals that "while at other levels of education the teacher is well identified, in higher education it is assumed that their competence comes from their mastery of the area of knowledge in which they work". She also emphasizes the deficiencies that exist in public policies related to and directed at higher education, as does Cunha (2000) when he reports that:

> I have pointed out that the university has a very clear paradox in this area. At the same time that, through its degree courses, it claims that there is specific knowledge, appropriate for the teaching profession and legitimized by it in the diploma, it denies the existence of this knowledge when it comes to its own teachers (p.45).

In relation to the precarious way in which the training of teachers takes place Cunha and Zanchet (2010) apud Murillo (2004) tell us:

> [...] teachers generally only rely on their personal initiative and experience to build and develop their theories about teaching and student learning. Throughout their lives, they have internalized teaching models and routines which are updated when they face urgent situations where they have to take on the role of teacher without anyone or anything having prepared them (p.4).

According to Soares and Cunha (2010), the lack of pedagogical knowledge limits teachers' actions and causes a variety of problems in the teaching and learning process. He says that teachers often bring a great deal of experience acquired through study and research to their profession, but do not know how to transmit or share all this knowledge with their students, as they are unaware of practices and resources aimed at sharing knowledge, thus making their professional experience from another activity an almost non-existent variable in teaching.

We mustn't forget that the current conception of teaching is based on modern science, where rational, objective and systematic knowledge is advocated, to the detriment of pedagogical knowledge, which is flexible when dealing with human educational aspects. From this point of view, it ends up having as its premise the traditional teaching of transmitting knowledge to mature students who are only committed to assimilating it. In this sense, thinking about the processes involved in teaching is seen only as a gift, neglecting the formation of pedagogical knowledge and configuring a role in which:

> [...] there is a lack of awareness in practice that student learning is the central objective of undergraduate courses and that our work as teachers should focus not just on the teaching process, but on the teaching-learning process of students and not on the transmission of knowledge by teachers. As simple and only passers of knowledge, this role really is in crisis and, for some time now, outdated (MASETTO, 1998, p. 12).

According to Pimenta (2002), although university professors have significant experience in their field, or have a great deal of theoretical background, in general there is a lack of preparation and even a lack of scientific knowledge of what a teaching-learning process is. Pimenta (2002) adds that:

> Generally, teachers join departments that run approved courses, in which the subjects they will teach have already been established. They receive ready-made syllabuses, plan individually (...) the results obtained are not studied (...) they receive no guidance on planning processes (...). As you can see, the issue of teaching at university goes beyond classroom processes, and calls into question the aims of undergraduate teaching, which has been recognized in different countries. (excerpt).

In fact, it's worth asking who is a university professor? They are intellectuals who will carry out teaching activities and be teachers in different situations, in different environments, in public and private schools. They can be scientists, researchers or technicians (OCTAVIO, 1986).

Masetto (1998) tells us that teaching in higher education has never been thought of as an activity of great importance:

> Firstly, training for university teaching has historically been a minor activity. Initially, there was a concern with good professional performance, and professional training, it was believed, could be given by anyone who knew how to do a particular job well. It was believed (as some still do today) that "anyone who knew how to

do things would automatically know how to teach", and there were no deeper concerns about the need for teachers to be pedagogically prepared (MASETTO, 1998, p. 11).

In the first instance, preventive planning is needed to avoid mistakes and incorporate new models into the initial training period, preventing an increase in the number of maladjusted teachers. With the changing role of the teacher and changes in the social context and interpersonal relationships at the teaching level, we are forced to rethink the initial training period. Future teachers are not ill-prepared, it's just that no one has made them aware of the important role they have to play in class dynamics and organization.

The Brazilian university is currently failing to fulfill a number of social functions that are its own and non-transferable. One of these functions, the training of teachers, needs to be quickly revived, otherwise the efforts to build democracy in the country will be frustrated (MENEZES, 1986).

It is necessary for universities to emphasize the training of teaching professionals with a vision of the totality of education and professional support related to the educational process. In this sense, teacher training must be based on the principles of the pedagogical project which make explicit the importance of linking theory and practice, the socio-political nature of education and an understanding of the global nature of the pedagogical process (MARAFON, 2005).

In his studies, Menezes (1986, p.118) shows us the real function of the educator and his role as a social agent:

The teacher doesn't have to be a mere teacher of things. They are a social agent of continuity, in other words, they don't have to be a pawn of an ideological state apparatus that would be here simply to reproduce schemes of oppression, etc. It is possible to think of the teacher as an agent for transforming society, in which he or she is not as he or she would like to be. In this way, they act not as isolated missionaries, but as part of the social effort.

With regard to the training of teachers at higher education level, it can be said that there is no specific legislation on the training of university teachers in Brazil. According to the current Parecer 977/65, which regulates stricto sensu postgraduate courses in Brazil, it states in a very general way that one of the aims of these programs is to train competent teachers for higher education. Talking about the competent training of this teacher, we can also infer that within this same opinion, there is a concept of teacher training focused on research:

> [...] to meet the quantitative expansion of our higher education, while ensuring that current quality levels are raised; to stimulate the development of scientific research by adequately preparing researchers; and to ensure the effective training of technicians and intellectual workers of the highest standard to meet the needs of national development in all sectors (SOARES CUNHA, 2010 p. 18).

The National Education Guidelines and Bases Law - LDBN (Law 9394/96) states in article 52, chapter II, that "[...] at least one third of the teaching staff must have a master's or doctorate degree [...]". As far as we can see, this law only specifies the number of teachers who must work in universities and the type of training these professionals must have (masters or doctorates). Neither law specifies how this training should take place, nor what set of skills it should contain.

The growing discussions about quality in higher education may reflect some deficient aspects in the teaching-learning process, since this quality is limited to the initial training of the teacher and little has been invested in continuing training, either because of the cost involved or because of the lack of projects that go beyond what has been proposed so far or adequate planning that takes into account the implementation of proposals that should be developed within a certain timeframe.

The rescue of the teacher's professional role by understanding the complexity of pedagogical practice and teaching knowledge, highlighting the importance of thinking about training not only in the academic dimension, but also in other times and spaces, has been significantly studied in recent decades (NUNES, 2001). In this sense, Garcia tells us that

> Professional development is a career-long development from initial training, induction, to continuing professional development throughout one's career [...]. Professional development is continuous, interactive, cumulative learning that combines a variety of learning formats. (1999, p. 27)

With another author (Tardif, 2002), we understand that the teacher's knowledge has a broader dimension than that built up in the Initial Training course. This knowledge emerges from the family environment, basic school, personal culture and

Continuing Education. The author points out that this wide range of knowledge involved in teacher training requires the ability to master it, integrate it and mobilize it, directing it towards one's own practice. This knowledge has a plural, heterogeneous and temporal character, since it is built up throughout life and career, and therefore also occurs in a particularized way in the experience of pedagogical practice in the exercise of teaching and not only in Initial Training in an institutionalized way during the student experience.

Because of this gap in initial training that many teachers have, Ribas tells us that:

> Ongoing training is essential for teachers to keep up to date in the area of knowledge in which they work, and also because of the very nature of pedagogical knowledge which, since it comes from the realm of praxis, is historical and unfinished (...). Pedagogical praxis is based on human and historical knowledge, which is therefore fractional, incomplete and provisional. It can therefore only be grasped through continuous research and study (2002, p. 47).

Continuing training is also justified not only by the shortcomings of initial teacher training courses, but also by the current situation in which schools find themselves and the challenges that need to be overcome. We must understand here that the teacher's training is completed in their daily practice in the classroom. Through this confrontation with reality, teachers acquire the necessary skills to reflect on the educational act and their methodological practices, changing them if necessary.

We can say that continuing education is an important way for teachers to reevaluate their teaching practice. It can be used as an environment to build up different types of knowledge, to rethink and redo the teacher's practice, reorganizing their skills and producing new knowledge.

In the next chapter we will look at the continuing education of university teachers and how this can make a significant contribution to improving learning and the quality of higher education.

Chapter II

CONTINUING EDUCATION AS TEACHER QUALIFICATION

Concern about teacher training is evident from the number of publications in this area. One of the main concerns in this regard is the growing number of new entrants to higher education.

This concern is justified by the fact that since the beginning of the history of education in Brazil, we can see that much thought has been given to the quantity of access to education rather than the quality of that education in schools and other educational spaces. And today this universalization is taking place within universities. Balzan tells us that:

> A major transformation has taken place in higher education worldwide in recent years. Its strong expansion, in quantitative terms, more marked in highly industrialized countries, but also present in developing countries, is generating new problems that we feel unprepared to face as educators: a modernity that has traditionally been characterized by elite education is being transformed at an accelerated pace into mass education. This fact, which is undoubtedly an achievement, presents us with problems that are characterized as real challenges: how can we reconcile mass education with teaching excellence? (...). From a didactic point of view, the problem lies in the search for a type of

> organization of teaching-learning situations capable of maintaining and even improving the levels of teaching efficiency and, at the same time, offering it to a large number of students. (BALZAN, 1997, p.8).

Higher education today has an increasingly heterogeneous public, many of whom are unprepared to enter higher education, making it necessary for teachers to know how to deal with cultural diversities that didn't exist before. And when we talk about teacher training, we can't forget that initial training is the first step towards this. This training needs to have the basic elements so that the future educator can put them to use in the learning of their students

For many thinkers such as Imbernon (2005), teacher training should be based on establishing strategies for thinking, perceiving, stimulating and focusing on decision-making in order to process, systematize and communicate information.

Emphasizing the above statement about teacher training and the role of higher education institutions, Marafon (2005, p.25) tells us that:

> Among its objectives, higher education should provide critical training through teaching and research, enabling professional action committed to explaining and overcoming social contradictions. Pedagogues who are aware that their practice is political will perceive the true intentions of plans, laws and educational planning, and that their work must aim at personal and social awareness and liberation. Today, we can say that the training of university lecturers has focused on their increasing specialization within one area of knowledge. "There

has been little concern about the pedagogical training of masters and doctors from the country's various postgraduate courses. Undergraduates have been 'fed' by qualified teachers, but without the slightest pedagogical competence". (VASCONCELOS, 1998, p. 86).

Teaching at higher education level requires that the teacher is competent and has mastered a specific area of knowledge through professional experience in the field, a mastery generally acquired through bachelor's degrees at universities and/or colleges and a few years of professional practice, i.e. that they already have a certain mastery of what they will be working with from this initial training.

Imbernon (2005) refers to the initial training of teachers as the professional knowledge of initiation into the profession, i.e. at this stage the acquisition of basic professional knowledge takes place. From this perspective, he goes on to say that: "[...] the structure of initial training must enable a global analysis of educational situations [...]" (p. 62) and promote interdisciplinary experiences that allow the future professional to integrate the knowledge and procedures of the various disciplines. This thought is clearly evident in the same author's speech:

> In order to assimilate basic professional knowledge, the training curriculum should promote interdisciplinary experiences that allow the future teacher to integrate the knowledge and procedures of the various disciplines with a psychopedagogical vision [...]. And this will be achieved by facilitating the discussion of themes, by reflecting on and confronting notions, attitudes, educational

realities, etc., in short, by analyzing pedagogical situations that lead them to propose, clarify, clarify and redefine concepts, to influence the formation or modification of attitudes, stimulating the capacity for analysis and criticism and activating sensitivity to current issues (IMBERNON, 2005, p. 62).

Another aspect raised by the same author in relation to initial training is that those who train teachers always act as a kind of hidden curriculum for educational methodology. Thus, there is a natural tendency for teachers to reproduce schemes or images of teaching.

This and other shortcomings in initial training can be remedied or alleviated by continuing to study, because as Imbernon (2006) argues, the teaching profession requires people to continue studying throughout their professional lives.

In the current context in which Brazilian education finds itself, it has become necessary to make forms, methods, didactics, times and new spaces more flexible. It also requires new teacher training, new ways of teaching and new ways of learning. All of this will have to be thought out and converted into new teaching-learning processes where technological training combined with distance higher education are the means by which we can meet the demands of the new millennium on education and society.

We mustn't forget that various profound changes in personal and cultural values and beliefs have marked today's society and the university is part of this system. Higher education is an integral part of the history of Brazilian society and is a stable and lasting social institution, conceived on the basis of society's norms and values. It is necessary to rethink both the training offered to future university teachers and the restructuring of the way in which knowledge is conceived in relation to the changes in technological advances that have been taking place in the contemporary world, making it necessary to think of a new way of teaching and learning. Teachers need to think of themselves as "participants in the unveiling of the world and the construction of rules for living with more wisdom and more pleasure" (CASTANHO, 2000, p. 87).

Knowledge, culture and good professional and intellectual training are important values in themselves, regardless of their practical applications and market value. Generally speaking, however, society recognizes and rewards competence that generates quality products and services, whether through the market or through governments and social and cultural organizations. There is no incompatibility between a broad education, which strengthens and stimulates the capacity for reflection and critical thinking, and qualification for productive work in all its aspects (SCHWARTZMAN, 2007).

The possibility of continuing to train and improve their didactic-pedagogical approach favors the optimistic view that these subjects have of their profession and, consequently, of themselves, emphasizing that the teachers, although they have not yet effectively transformed their practices, demonstrate the possibility of doing so, thus evidencing the search for a reflective posture. We can say that the construction of shared pedagogical knowledge presupposes the creation of a network of interactions and mediations capable of enhancing the teacher's reflective process.

When we think of continuing education, we are referring to teaching training for competent, participative and critical professionals who are inserted into the university community as agents of change.

In view of this, it is necessary for continuing training to provide teachers with new knowledge, understanding that this training is more than the acquisition of techniques and knowledge, it is the key moment for socialization and professional configuration. This training should generate attitudes that encourage permanent updating. According to Lampert (1998, p. 24) *"Practice should be at the center of teacher training, allowing experience to be interpreted, reinterpreted and systematized. "*

It is important to emphasize that teachers can be more successful in their classroom teaching if they have had experience in the field, if they are able to present and implement different proposals throughout the course, and if they exchange procedures with their peers.

In this sense, Garcia, quoting Menges (1988), points out some elements that should be considered in the professional development of university teachers. This development refers to theory and practice that facilitates improvement in the teacher's role in a variety of domains, including intellectual, institutional, personal, social and pedagogical. For the author, professional development only makes sense if it is interrelated with the development of the institution. When we look at what the LDBN says about education professionals, we see that it makes sense to intertwine these two elements, because by carrying out their teaching duties, they enable the institution to develop too.

For Libaneo (2004), continuous training consists of training sessions within the working day, organized by the institution through management and pedagogical coordination, and outside the working day. It takes the form of study, reflection, discussion and confrontation of teachers' experiences, and teachers and the institution are responsible for this training.

Talking about continuing and in-service training, it is important to emphasize that it should combine theory and practice so that the professional can see how the whole process takes place.

educational process. In this sense, Marafon (2001, p.9) tells us:

> This training was based on the principles of the Pedagogical Project, which emphasized the importance of linking theory and practice, the socio-political nature of education and an understanding of the global nature of the pedagogical process. This led to an emphasis on training professionals with a vision of the totality of education and the professional actions related to the educational process.

According to Freire (1983, p. 20): [...] The more I train myself as a professional, the more I systematize my experiences, the more I make use of cultural heritage, which is everyone's heritage and which everyone must serve, the more my responsibility towards men increases.

Geglio (2006) points out in his study on issues of continuing teacher training that teachers almost always criticize the continuing training courses they attend, mainly because they are too theoretical. For this author, the teachers' request is for the courses to be more practical, because what they believe they need is practice and not theory, which often ends up being very boring.

In this context, the same author points out the importance of the interaction between theory and practice, where one cannot be submissive to the other. He concludes that teachers' tendency to give more value to practice leads them to pragmatism, which distorts the transformative relationship of teaching practice, as it acquires the concept of: "[...] functional, which is established by immediate doing [...]" (GEGLIO, 2006, p. 81).

This combination of theory and practice is fundamental if the university is to make progress towards improving the quality of its students' learning and consequently the results of external evaluations.

Another important point to be addressed is that professionals in education should not end their training within the confines of a degree course, but should be part of this changing world and rethink the demands of contemporaneity. After entering the job market, this professional needs to return to university to further study theoretical issues that have emerged from within their pedagogical practice or to carry out new research, thus becoming a professional of excellence, which is what our society demands in terms of higher education teachers.

In the next chapter, we'll look at the quality of higher education, highlighting the role of teacher training as one of the factors in improving university assessment indices.

Chapter III

IMPROVING THE QUALITY OF HIGHER EDUCATION

"But the concept of quality is not static, there is no consensus on its meaning, nor is there a single model, because it depends on the idea of training and teaching. For a long time, and because it comes from the world of production, quality was interpreted as an absolute concept, close to the dimensions of innate and attribute of a product. In recent times, quality in education has been analyzed from the student's point of view, from how they perceive it, but unlike conservative positions that introduce performance indicators to prove the quality of a process, it is seen as a trend, as a trajectory, as a process of continuous construction" (IMBERNON, 2006).

Throughout the history of Brazilian education, we have been faced with a less than optimistic reality regarding the quality of education in our country. Due to the universalization of education, which has not been accompanied by quality, what was supposed to guarantee teaching and learning for the most excluded has become a point of concern for the government and society as a whole. It is worth remembering here that the ideal of school for all was not the villain for the low performance of Brazilian education, but rather the lack of concern about improving the quality of teaching offered in both the public and private education sectors.

Although Brazil has improved its ranking in the latest PISA, we are still a long way from reaching the levels expected of 1st world countries. To try to raise the quality of Brazilian education, the MEC has set itself some audacious targets within the PNE. Of course, this is a long-term effort, and one that combines efforts at the federal, state and municipal levels to boost education in the country and reduce regional inequalities.

The new goals of the PNE (2011-2020) range from the eradication of illiteracy; the universalization of school attendance, overcoming educational inequalities, improving the quality of teaching, training for work, promoting socio-environmental sustainability, promoting the humanistic, scientific and technological development of the country, establishing a target for the application of public resources to education as a proportion of gross domestic product, valuing education professionals and even spreading the principles of equity, respect for diversity and the democratic management of education.

Despite the changes that need to be made by the government, we know that the basis for change in the education system, and consequently in society, lies in the university itself. To do this, we need to get society as a whole to participate in the process that will define the needs and guidelines of the educational system that will transform the reality of our country.

The initial step for these changes to take place is to demand higher quality in higher education, through its different components, and in this sense UNESCO (1999) tells us that:

> The demand for quality has become an essential concern in higher education. Its ability to meet the needs and expectations of society ultimately depends on the quality of staff, programs and students, but also on the infrastructure and university

environment. The demand for "quality" has many aspects and the primary objective of the measures implemented to this end must be to improve institutions as much as the system as a whole. (UNESCO, Change and Development in Higher Education, 1999 p. 9, XV).

3.1- External Evaluations

Before we talk about external evaluations, their procedures and uses, it is necessary to talk a little about what evaluation is and its purpose within the teaching and learning process.

According to Vasconcellos (2000), evaluation is a comprehensive process of human existence, which implies a critical reflection on practice, in order to capture its advances, its resistances, its difficulties and enable a decision to be made on what to do to overcome the problems identified or obstacles.

According to Luckesi (1999), the assessment that is practiced at school is the assessment of guilt, and grades are used to justify the need to classify students, where performances are compared and not the objectives that are to be achieved. The core function of assessment is to help the student learn and the teacher teach, while also determining how much and at what level the objectives are being achieved (Perrenoud, 1999). This requires the use of appropriate assessment instruments and procedures (Libaneo, 1994, p.204).

In Luckesi's (1999) view, "in order not to be authoritarian and conservative, evaluation has the task of being diagnostic, that is, it must be the dialectical instrument of progress, it must be the instrument for identifying new directions". For the author, assessment should verify learning not only from the minimum possible, but from the minimum necessary. He also stresses the importance of criteria, as assessment cannot be practiced using data invented by the teacher, although the definition of these criteria is not fixed and immutable, but changes according to the needs of students and teachers.

We can say that the forms of education, which in turn are made explicit in educational theories, pedagogical theories, stem from the way in which human existence is produced. It is these theories that underpin methodological procedures, including assessment practices.

Assessment, solely as an instrument of measurement, a hallmark of positivism, hides and mystifies more than it shows, or points to what needs to be taken up again, worked on again and in a different way, and what is essential for the student to know. Nor can we forget the instruments used to assess (confused with measurement), which underpin this decision-making process and require questioning, not only as to their design, but also as to their coherence and appropriateness with what has been worked on in the classroom and the way in which what is to be assessed has been worked on (COLETIVO DE AUTORES, 1992 p. 103).

Saviani (2000) states that the path to knowledge should be to ask questions within the student's everyday life and culture; rather than teaching and learning knowledge, it needs to be put into practice in everyday life, questioning, answering, evaluating, in a work carried out by groups and individuals who build their world and do it for themselves. When we evaluate a higher education course, we want to know how effective it is; we want to know if it is working within the expectations we have for the training of professionals.

We are analyzing variables, taken for granted, that measure the quality of the education offered. These variables are supposed to have already been tested and can offer us a good margin of safety in our evaluation. However, this variety in the standards used to measure evaluation has its limits, and the information we need can only be concluded by analyzing the whole process, which has not been the case.

In this sense, HARVEY and NEWTON (2004) tell us that one point subject to debate is the role of quality control in higher education through external evaluations, and question how these act to inhibit or legitimize the expected changes.

As far as higher education is concerned, we can say that the oldest Brazilian experience with aspects of evaluation is that of postgraduate studies in the strict sense, which has been carried out by CAPES since 1976. However, due to demands from international funding agencies such as the World Bank (IBRD) and the International Monetary Fund (IMF), evaluation mechanisms were created at all levels of education during the Fernando Henrique Cardoso government: in basic education with the SAEB (Sistema de Avaliapao da Educapao Basica), in secondary education with the ENEM (Exame Nacional do Ensino Medio) and in higher education with the Exame Nacional de Cursos (Provao).

In recent years, INEP has had the role of reorganizing the system of statistical surveys and has had evaluations at practically all educational levels as its central activity. MEC/INEP currently carries out the Evaluation of Degree Courses in order to recognize or renew degree courses, which is a necessary measure for issuing diplomas.

During the Lula government, a commission was set up to propose a new model for evaluating Brazilian higher education. It was only in April 2004, by means of Law No. 10.861, that the National Higher Education Evaluation System (SINAES) was created, whose function would be to evaluate all the aspects that revolve around the axes: teaching, research, extension, social responsibility, student performance, institution management, teaching staff, facilities, among other aspects.

The aim of SINAES is to ensure a national evaluation process for higher education institutions, degree courses and the academic performance of their students, in accordance with article 9, paragraphs VI, VIII and IX, of the National Education Guidelines and Bases Law:

VI - ensure a national process for evaluating school performance in primary, secondary and higher education, in collaboration with the education systems, with the aim of defining priorities and improving the quality of teaching;

VIII - ensure a national evaluation process for higher education institutions, with the cooperation of the systems responsible for this level of education;

IX - to authorize, recognize, accredit, supervise and evaluate, respectively, the courses of higher education institutions and the establishments of its education system. (CNE/Law No. 9394, 1996.)

At the beginning of the 1990s, INEP acted as a funder of academic work focused on education. From 1995 onwards, the organization was restructured. With the reorganization of the sector responsible for statistical surveys, it was intended that educational information could, in fact, guide the formulation of policies by the Ministry of Education.

Evaluations of institutions would then be at the heart of the evaluation process, covering, among other things, improving the quality of higher education, guiding the expansion of its offer, permanently increasing its institutional efficiency and academic and social effectiveness and, especially, the promotion of the deepening of the social commitments and responsibilities of higher education institutions, through the valorization of their public mission, the promotion of democratic values, respect for difference and diversity, the affirmation of autonomy and institutional identity.

Evaluations of undergraduate courses, on the other hand, are a procedure used by the MEC to recognize or renew the recognition of undergraduate courses, and are currently a necessary measure for issuing diplomas. This evaluation is now carried out periodically in order to comply with the provisions of the Higher Education Guidelines and Bases Law, with the aim of guaranteeing the quality of teaching offered by Higher Education Institutions.

In relation to these external evaluations and the role of the MEC in this process, MACEDO (2007) tells us that when analyzing the performance of the MEC in the process of evaluating, regulating and monitoring Brazilian higher education, it is necessary to bear in mind the complexity and difficulties of carrying out this task in a country with the continental dimensions of Brazil and which requires great cultural, socio-economic and educational diversity, and that this situation is aggravated by two other factors: Firstly, because the culture of systematized evaluation is very recent in Brazil, and secondly, because of the growing expansion of Brazilian higher education, which occurred mainly in the 1990s.

The same author tells us that this expansion was necessary, but it was carried out in a disorganized way, without planning because it wasn't planned, which obviously led to a series of consequences and complicated the MEC's ability to carry out its evaluation, monitoring and regulation functions properly. The author believes that this situation has been aggravated by other factors of a conceptual, operational and economic nature, which have guided the process of evaluating, monitoring and regulating higher education, and that it needs to be improved, with most of the problems stemming from changes in legislation that often bring no benefit to the system.

Other factors pointed out by the same author are: the excessive regulatory control exercised by the MEC over private universities; the inadequacy of the evaluation instruments, which need to be improved and refined; the lack of synergy, coordination and definition of the attributions and competencies of the MEC's structures; the need for the National Education Council to act as a state body, trying not to exercise government functions and the existence of a prejudice against the private higher education system, a prejudice that is not the MEC's, it is not the government's, it is a prejudice that is ingrained in the different structures that promote the evaluation and monitoring of the system.

Another point highlighted by the author is the evaluation of teaching conditions carried out by Inep's *on-site* evaluation committees. In the author's view, these committees are mostly made up of staff recruited from public universities, without the necessary experience in the process of comparative analysis and with little experience in the reality of private education.

Another negative factor is the inadequacy of the forms, which are flawed, not very discriminating and with inadequate scores to be assigned to the different evaluation items, which leads to contradictory results, i.e. often the sum of the points assigned, the sum of the values assigned to the different items analyzed presents a mathematical result that is totally different from the evaluation that the evaluator makes, which is subjective, but is a global evaluation that reflects reality.

For this evaluation to become equitable, the author says, the following measures should be adopted, among others:

- Promote the stability of the standards and procedures used for evaluation, trying not to change them all the time;

- Improve coordination and cooperation between SESU and Inep;

- Review evaluation instruments, seeking to improve them;

- Accredit the CNE as an appeals body;

- Promote the training of Inep's team of evaluators;

- Rediscuss the length of the course recognition and accreditation periods for HEIs, so that they are not shortened;

- Inep will recruit a larger number of assessors, as long as they are qualified in the private sector;

- Create an independent agency for the accreditation and certification of HEIs;

- To resolve the ambiguity of the MEC's role as the maintainer of the public system and simultaneously the evaluator of the federal education system, then at the moment we have to prove that a public institution is not adequate, the private institution has to prove that it complies with the legislation and that it provides quality education;

3.2- The Role of Teachers in the Quality of Higher Education

As we well know, today's society is undergoing a series of changes. The act of teaching is becoming a new challenge for educators every day. Within this new society of technology, information and globalization, teachers do not see themselves ready to teach their students competently, since those who have the role of teaching must be aware of the new demands and problems that arise in the classroom and be prepared for these new challenges.

In this sense, an important factor if educators are to be able to cope competently with these challenges is their initial and ongoing training. We know that the initial training of our educators often fails to prepare them in a way that enables them to act fully within this society of such rapid transformation.

We must also remember that we are never fully trained, which is why it is so important for these teachers to receive ongoing, in-service training so that we can achieve a better quality of education.

The quality of education has been one of the concerns of those who manage education for decades and is the subject of contemporary educational policies such as the Federal Constitution (88) and the LDB (9394/96). Article 61 of the LDB 96 makes it clear that: *"The training of education professionals in order to meet the objectives of the different levels and modalities of education and the characteristics of each stage of the student's development will be based on:*

- *Linking theory and practice, including through in-service training;*
- *Drawing on previous training and experience in educational institutions and other activities".*

We can say that the foundations of teacher training are based on the theory-practice relationship, noting that the quality of teaching is directly linked to the teacher's initial and continuing training.

It should be emphasized here that a policy that guarantees the quality of higher education needs to go through a process in which teachers are a fundamental part of bringing about change within the university, considering their role as an integral part of improving the quality of this educational establishment. In order to achieve this quality objective, it is of the utmost importance to identify the competency profiles and attitudes of these professionals before defining selection criteria. In this sense, UNESCO, in its documents, tells us that:

> A quality assurance policy therefore requires identifying the required profiles of skills and attitudes, before defining a selection policy for teachers and researchers based essentially on merit, and applying it rigorously. But it also means managing careers in such a way that there is a constant match between the needs to be met, which evolve over time, and the available profiles of skills and attitudes, which requires policies for the ongoing training of teachers and researchers and, consequently, strategies for strengthening them. (UNESCO 1989, p.136)

The same document stresses the importance, as a guarantee of the quality of higher education, of working on the personal motivation of these professionals, giving them an appropriate social and financial status. It also looks at the pedagogical training of these teachers, leading them to adopt more innovative teaching concepts and methods.

Reflection on one's own practice becomes even more urgent when we see a certain mismatch between initial training and this need.

> [...] as much as they have specific knowledge for practice, there is a gap in the development of a reflective capacity for undergraduates about their own practice. Reflective processes

are denied, since the curriculum has a terminal structure, with internships at the end of the course, making it impossible to reflect later in other parts of the training process (BERNARDI; SANCHOTENE; MOLINA, 2010, p. 1).

For all the policies for the professional qualification of educators to come to fruition, it is necessary for managers to consider the level of training of teachers, to identify the quality of their professional practices by observing pedagogical practice; the evaluation of projects; classroom organization; mastery of strategies; management of content; the ability to produce pedagogical knowledge and develop skills. The training aims to contribute to the teacher's ability to continue learning responsibly (PARENTE, 2007, 23).

Continuing training, understood not just as an organized process of updating in the light of a diversified teaching career, but as a process that encompasses the critical-reflective dimension, which understands the teacher as a historically situated subject and articulates scientific and pedagogical knowledge and teaching experiences, in order to promote the professional autonomy that comes from the permanent appropriation of knowledge and interaction with other subjects in the educational process (FALSARELLA, 2004). Analyzing continuing teacher training, Carvalho (2003, p. 17) argues:

> The expression continuing education, being much broader than the word course, brings to our reflection, albeit inadvertently, a more complex idea of the timeline and succession of events. If we want to use this expression to reinforce the idea of continuity,

> we will necessarily have other elements on our agenda that also evoke chronological notions, starting points, ruptures, simultaneities, histories, programs, chronologies, etc. [...] perhaps we can understand this current emergence of the need for continuing education as a good opportunity to look for more meaningful paths in the relationship between academic production and basic education.

Today, we can say that technological training meets the needs that the construction of this Society imposes and contributes as a response to the stimuli and demands of the various stakeholders in this construction. This is justified by the fact that these courses are geared towards application in line with the world of work. Their curricular organization is based on the principles of flexibility, interdisciplinarity and contextualization. The possibility of structuring curricula in modules provides not only greater flexibility in their design, so that they are in tune with the demands of the productive sector, but also contributes to broadening and speeding up the meeting of the needs of workers, companies and society.

Based on this assumption, distance education is a facilitator in this process of acquiring training for work and society, as it breaks down spatial and temporal distances and enables interactivity through various resources. It is important to remember here that in order for these distance learning courses to be of high quality, it is necessary to ensure that the teachers at these colleges are in tune with the world of technology, as well as being trained in methodologies and forms of knowledge specific to this modality, which today serves thousands of people in search of professional qualifications. It is therefore important to constantly update, renew and restructure courses and curricula in line with the demands of the world of work.

We've just talked about the role of universities in the continuing education of teachers, but we also need to talk about the role of this teacher inside and outside the university, because we can't forget that the continuous search for new knowledge is one of the driving forces behind economic development and one of the main points of education. In this sense, the university lecturer will have to look for alternatives in the search for knowledge in order to remain capable of developing new skills to be able to meet the continuous demands and challenges imposed by the job market.

It's worth pointing out that in order to have a teaching profession that is committed to quality education allied to the university's objectives, it's essential for educators to have initial training and pedagogical support throughout their careers, taking into account aspects that, as they develop their profession, are punctuated. In this context, we can say that this is the aim of university pedagogy, which advocates scientific training allied to teaching practice from the outset.

The idea that university teaching goes beyond passing on scientific knowledge implies teaching responsibility and a commitment to the quality of teaching, methods, attitudes and professionalism. Quality training for university teachers is the basis for reflections such as these throughout their careers. Another point to highlight is the institutional support offered to teachers, which makes it possible to share ideas, support and reflections.

It has become important for higher education institutions to think of discussion forums as a way of supporting and encouraging the development of teaching careers. A space in which teaching practice can be reflected on and discussed, where university professors, together with other professors, can share difficulties, advances, knowledge and values (BEHRENS, 1998). This process ends up contributing to the realization of the university's own commitment to the theoretical and practical development of future professionals who will act in the society of which they are a part.

Higher education professionals who don't keep up with technological developments and changes in mentality and behavior run the risk of becoming obsolete. Today's educational institutions require professionals who can interpret, elaborate, transform and be creative - people with knowledge.

In the following chapter, we'll take a look at the research, the means by which it was carried out and the way in which it was structured throughout the work.

Chapter IV

THE RESEARCH

The meaning and *status of* the word methodology has varied over the years. Since it has no status of its own, it needs to be defined within a theoretical-methodological context. Within this context, the role of the researcher is to interpret the reality being researched, analyzing it according to the tools provided by their theoretical-epistemological stance.

According to Alves-Mazzoti and Gewandsznajder (2000), the main characteristic of qualitative research is the search for understanding and interpretation, based on the assumption that people act according to their beliefs, perceptions, feelings and values, so that behavior always has a meaning and sense that cannot be known immediately, which requires an investigative attitude of unveiling.

Teixeira (1997), based on the contributions of Liidke and Andre (1986), emphasizes that this approach seeks to understand by means of apprehending the specificities of the phenomena addressed within the context of the context in which they occur. It also emphasizes the search to break the dichotomy between subject and object of knowledge, as it recognizes the inseparability between the objective world and the subject's subjectivity. For Lidke and Andre (1986) there is a greater concern with the process than with the product of the research, so that the researcher's interest lies in understanding how the phenomenon studied manifests itself.

Alves-Mazzoti and Gewandsznajder (2000) point out that qualitative research is flexible and marked by diversity, and does not support precise rules that can be applied to all cases. Therefore, we can say that this research project is characterized as a systematic research plan, without it being a fixed reference that cannot be questioned or reformulated in the course of its execution.

According to Liidke and Andre (1986), in order to carry out research it is necessary to promote a confrontation between the data, the evidence, the information collected on a given subject and the theoretical knowledge accumulated about it. It's about building up a body of knowledge. This knowledge is not only the fruit of the researcher's curiosity, restlessness, intelligence and investigative activity, but also the continuation of what has been developed and systematized by those who have worked on the subject before. The first stage in the process of preparing a piece of research is to determine its subject.

The methodology used was bibliographical research, the aim of which is to put the researcher in direct contact with everything that has been said and written on the subject.

It can be said that bibliographic research is the search for a problematization of the research project based on published references, analyzing and discussing cultural and scientific contributions. This is an excellent technique for providing the researcher with theoretical background, knowledge and scientific training.

4.1 Material

The material used to carry out this research was limited to the bibliographical research mentioned below. The methodology chosen was to apply the critical method to the arguments found and the inductive-deductive method to systematize the information gathered. A bibliographic survey was carried out, collecting data through approximately 30 books, on the following themes: continuing education in higher education, the history of higher education, external evaluation in higher education, among other related themes. Other materials used were electronic scientific articles and scientific journals, scientific papers related to the themes of this research.

4.2 Procedure

At this stage, the focus was on a careful reading of the bibliographic material. From this reading, comments, citations, summaries and personal observations useful for the development of the academic work were systematically constructed by means of notes and cards. After analyzing the bibliographical references and the foundations of truth in the statements offered, the content found in the respective books, articles, scientific papers and other materials researched on the object of study, this research was organized and synthesized, so that the information presented could be related to each other and maintain a cohesion to enable better reading.

FINAL CONSIDERATIONS

The aim of this study is to investigate the type of professional training and qualification undertaken by teachers in higher education and how this influences the quality of teaching. Through a history of teacher training from its beginnings to the present day, investigating how teachers have been qualifying, as well as analyzing how this training reflects directly or indirectly on improving the quality of higher education, analyzing the bibliography on the subject to understand how professional qualification occurs among these higher education teachers.

We can say that the current context requires teachers to be in constant training, permeated by the multiple aspects that the complex nature of society demands. Silva (2000, p. 91), when talking about the Portuguese reality of teacher training as a right and a duty, already listed three fundamental objectives:

> To improve the professional competence of teachers in the various areas of their activity; - To encourage teachers to participate actively in educational innovation and in improving the quality of education and teaching; - To acquire new skills related to the specialization required by the differentiation and modernization of the education system.

One of the ways for professionals to improve the way they teach is to evaluate their own practice. We must understand that educational practice, seen as a means of transforming teachers, helps them to reflect and improve their teaching. In this sense, research should be another tool used by teachers to improve their teaching, so that they can use theory to improve their educational practice.

By evaluating his or her own practice, the teacher is transforming it to benefit a more qualified education for his or her students. Reflecting on this practice benefits both the teacher and the student, as the teacher will analyze the lessons he or she has taught and think of ways to modify them for the benefit of the student.

There are many issues that need to be analyzed in order to reach a final conclusion on what is really important for quality in higher education. We know that there are many problems, but we are only one step away from discovering the causes of this gap in quality. For now, we just need to emphasize the importance of continuing teacher training, as a guide to the teaching and learning process, and reflection on teaching and learning practices, against the backdrop of the objectives set out in the context of each university. In addition to analyzing the assessment objectives and instruments, we will understand what they are for and who they are for.

We must not forget here that we need to analyze the results of these external evaluations, promoted by the MEC, from a diagnostic point of view, where they can be valuable instruments for the educational changes that are so long awaited, instead of being punitive instruments that do not achieve what is really necessary. It is worth remembering that these external indicators are not enough to evaluate the entire teaching and learning process, which is very complex. However, by analyzing the results achieved, universities can improve their pedagogical work and better define their goals, with a view to achieving social quality.

It is therefore believed that improving the quality of higher education can be boosted by research that informs the development of more comprehensive educational policies, whose measures enable actions to be taken that involve various aspects, including those mentioned above: continuing education for educators, their professional knowledge and skills, reorganizing their skills and producing new knowledge.

This essay has highlighted the concern with valuing and encouraging continuing training for teachers in higher education, from this perspective, seeking to meet the specific needs of each area, engaged in the university context as a whole, with pedagogical practice as its central object, offering teachers recognition of their productive capacity, in the experience of their own teaching action. It should be reiterated that the identity of the education professional can only be conceived by linking it to the meaning of social practice, so that throughout their training education professionals need to recognize themselves based on their insertion in an unequal society.

This study is not limited to the subject at hand, but it is hoped that it can contribute to a process of constant reflection and transformation for those who are committed to quality teaching in our universities.

REFERENCES

ALVES -MAZZOTI, A. J. and GEWANDSZNADJER, F. O metodo nas ciencias naturais e sociais: pesquisa quantitativa. 2ª ed. Sao Paulo: Pioneira Thomson Learding. 2002.

BALZAN, Newton Cesar. From the Student to the University Professor: paths to higher education didactics. Revista de Educagao, 1997.

BERNARDI, Guilherme Bardemaker; SANCHOTENE, Monica Urroz; MOLINA NETO, Vicente. Professional training and School Physical Education: contributions of the curriculum to teaching practice. Lecturas: Physical Education and Sports. Revista Digital, Buenos Aires, v. 14, n. 141, feb., 2010. Available at: <http://www.efdeportes.com/ efd141/formacao-profissional-e-educacao-fisica-escolar.htm>. Accessed on: 01 May 2010.

BRAZIL. Federal Education Council. Opinion No. 977/65. Definition of postgraduate courses. Brasilia, DF, 1965.

BRAZIL. *Decree-Law 8.530, of January 2,* 1946. 1946. Available at: <www.soleis.adv.br>. Accessed on: Jan. 16, 2009.

. Law 5.692/71, of August 11, 1971. *Diario Oficial da Uniao*, Brasilia, August 12, 1971.

BEHRENS, Marilda Aparecida. Pedagogical training and the challenges of the modern world. In: MASETTO, Marcos Tarciso (Org.). Teaching at university. Campinas, SP: Papirus, 1998, p. 57-68.

CARVALHO, A. M. P; GIL-PEREZ, D. Formação de professores de Ciencias: tendências e inovagoes. 6ª ed. Sao Paulo: Cortez, 2001.

CASTANHO, Sergio E. M. Educagao superior do sec. XXI: discutao de uma proposta. Caxambu: ANPED/2000.

AUTHORS' COLLECTIVE. *Methodology of physical education teaching.* Sao Paulo:

Cortez, 1992.

FALSARELLA, A. M. Formação continuada e pratica de sala de aula: os efeitos da formacao continuada na atuagao do professor. Sao Paulo: Autores Associados, 2004.

FREIRE, P. Educagao e Mudanga. 7ª ed. Rio de Janeiro: Paz e Terra, 1983.

GARCIA, Carlos Marcelo. Teacher training for educational change. Porto: Porto, 1999

GEGLIO, P. C. Questoes da formagao continuada de professores. Sao Paulo: Alfa-Omega, 2006.

GHIRALDELLI, J. P. Historia da educagao brasileira. Sao Paulo: Cortez, 2006.

HARVEY, L.; NEWTON, J. Transforming quality evaluation. Quality in Higher Education,Lodon, v. 10, n. 2, p. 149-165, jul. 2004

IMBERNON, F. Teacher and professional training: training for change and uncertainty. 5ª ed. Sao Paulo: Cortez, 2005.

NATIONAL INSTITUTE FOR EDUCATIONAL STUDIES AND RESEARCH - INEP. National Basic Education Assessment System (SAEB). New Perspectives. Brasilia, 2001.

LAMPERT, Ernani. University professor: initial and continuing training. Revista de Estudos Universitarios. Sorocaba, vol. 24, n° 1, June 1998. p. 17-35

LIBANEO, J. C. Organização e gestao da escola: teoria e pratica. 5ª ed. Goiania: Editora Alternativa, 2004.

LIBANEO, J.C. Pedagogia e pedagogos, para que? / 8§ . Ed. Sao Paulo: Cortez, 2005.

LIBANEO, J.C. Didatica. 10§ . ed. Sao Paulo: Cortez, 1994.

LUCKESI. C.C. Avaliagao da aprendizagem escolar. 9§ . ed.Sao Paulo: Cortez, 1999.

LUDKE, Menga; ANDRE, Marli E.D.A. Pesquisa em educagao: abordagens qualitativas. Sao Paulo: EPU, 1986.

MACEDO, A. R. de /Anais: FNESP: 8° forum nacional: ensino superior brasileiro: educação superior : questão de estado/ prioridade social Sindicato das entidades mantenedoras de estabelecimentos de ensino, SEMESP. - Rio de Janeiro, RJ: Corba editora Artes graficas LTDA. 2007.

MARAFON, M.R.C. Pedagogia Critica: uma metodologia na construgao do conhecimento: Petropolis, RJ: Vozes, 2001.

. Contribution of the Pedagogue and Pedagogy to Education: research and criticism. Campinas: Editora Alinea, 2005.

MASETTO, Marcos (org.). Teaching at the University. Campinas, SP: Papirus, 1998.

MAZZEU, F. J. C. Uma proposta metodológica para a formacao continuada de professores na perspectiva historico-social. *Cad. CEDES,* Apr. 1998, vol.19, no.44, p.59-72. ISSN 0101-3262

MOROSIN, Marilia. University teaching and the challenges of national reality.
National Institute for Educational Studies and Research, Brasilia: National Institute for Educational Studies and Research, n.2, p.11-21, 2000

NUNES, Celia Maria Fernandes. Teaching knowledge and teacher training: a brief overview of Brazilian research. Educagao & Sociedade, Campinas, n.74, p. 27-42, Apr., 2001.

OLIVEIRA, A.C.B. Qual a sua formacao, professor? Campinas, SP: Papirus, 1994 (Teacher training: Training and pedagogical work).

PARENTE, F.T. O papel da escola na formação do professor. In Gestao em rede. n° 80. Curitiba: Consed, September 2007

PIMENTA, Selma Garrido; ANASTASIOU, Lea das Gragas C. *Docencia no ensino superior*. Sao Paulo: Cortez, 2002.

PERRENOUD, P. Evaluation: from excellence to the regulation of learning. Porto Alegre: Artmed, 1999.

RIBAS, M. H. Construindo a Competência: processo de formacao de professores. Sao Paulo: Olho D'agua, 2002.

SAVIANI, D. Saber escolar, curriculo e didatica. 3T ed. Campinas: Autores Associados, 2000.

Teacher training: historical and theoretical aspects of the problem in the Brazilian context, in Revista Brasileira de Educacao v. 14 n. 40 jan./abr. 2009

SCHWARTZMAN, Simon. Towards a new higher education policy for Brazil. Oct, 2007. Available at <http://www.schwartzman.org.br/simon/comissao.htm>. Accessed 12/08/2011.

SILVA, A.M.C. A formagao continua de professores: uma reflexao sobre as praticas de reflexao em formagao. In: MENGA, Liidke et alii. *Revista Educagao & Sociedade*, ano XXI, n°. 72. p. 89- 109, 2000.
SOARES, Sandra Regina; CUNHA, Maria Isabel. Postgraduate programs in education: a training ground for university teaching? Revista Brasileira de Pos-graduação, Brasilia, v. 7, n.14, dec. 2010, p.577-604.

TARDIF, Maurice. Teaching knowledge and professional training. Petropolis: Vozes, 2002.

TEIXEIRA, M.A.R.M. Teacher: action and training - the search for a new professionalism. 1997. Dissertation (Master's Degree) - Pontifical Catholic University of Sao Paulo.

UNESCO. World Conference on Higher Education - Final Report. Paris: UNESCO. Vol. 1, 1998.

UNESCO. Trends in Higher Education for the 21st Century/UNESCO/Council of Rectors of Brazilian Universities: translation by Maria Beatriz Ribeiro de Oliveira Gongalves; illustration by Edson Fogaga - Brasilia: UNESCO/ CRUB, 1999. 720p.

VASCONCELOS, Maria Lucia M. Carvalho. Contributing to the training of university teachers. Campinas, SP: Papirus, 1998

. A formagao do professor do ensino superior. 2T ed. Sao Paulo: Pioneira, 2000

9 786208 325541